TABLE OF CONTENTS

To Teachers and Parents 4

Bible Wordles 5-8

Bible Rhymle 9, 10

Musical Connections 11, 12

Square Connections 13, 14

Wordle Epistle 15, 16

Hidden Names 17, 18

Common Connections 19, 20

Quantitative Connections 21-23

Alphabet Connections 24, 25

Cryptic Quotes 26, 27

Crucial Connections 28-30

Round About ''The Word'' 31-42

Answer Key 43-45

Awards 46-48

TO THE TEACHERS AND PARENTS

Words are the lifeblood of language! Although words are merely the combination of letters, they are one of the most powerful influences in our lives. Words are the tools of good thinking. They give us the opportunity to stretch our minds, expand our imaginations and allow us to experience playfulness.

BIBLE WORD FUN is intended to do all these things with words associated with the Bible. This collection of games, puzzles, codes and creative thinking and writing activities is designed to allow children the pleasure of working and playing with Bible-related words. These puzzles will also expand knowledge of Bible facts and sharpen Bible research skills.

We hope that this book will provide unlimited usage for classroom teachers, Sunday School teachers, youth directors, pastors, laymen and parents. Its usage is limited only by the imagination of the user. It can be used as an activity while traveling, as a teaching tool, as an enrichment activity, as a rainy day activity, at parties, as a warm-up or closing activity for Sunday School, as a youth group competition or as an indoor recess.

This book is suitable for use with upper elementary students, middle school students, junior high school students, high school students as well as adults. Each activity is presented as a separate entity. Activities are appropriate for independent use or in pairs, small groups or large groups. Hopefully, these materials will motivate the design and creation of other original word game activities that can be shared and utilized by creative thinkers to reinforce Bible facts in a new, exciting and challenging way.

BIBLE WORDLES

WORDLES are groups of words and letters written so that they stand for a familiar phrase. These BIBLE WORDLES are all hymn titles or phrases related to the Bible and Christian living. List your answers at the bottom of the page.

abide me

1.

THE BLOOD

2.

O' DAY

3.

STANDING THE PROMISES

4.

GRACE our sin

5.

ROCK

6.

1._____   2._____

3._____   4._____

5._____   6._____

BIBLE WORDLES

WORDLES are groups of words and letters written so that they stand for a familiar phrase. These BIBLE WORDLES are all hymn titles or phrases related to the Bible and Christian living. List your answers at the bottom of the page.

His GREAT love
His GREAT love

1.

1. Your Blessings
2. Your Blessings
3. Your Blessings
4. Your Blessings

2.

MY MY MY MY MY MY MY
MY   THERE RINGS   MY
MY   A   MY
MY   MELODY   MY
MY MY MY MY MY MY MY

3.

the Bells of Heaven

4.

GROUND

GROUND GROUND

5.

1. _____   2. _____

3. _____   4. _____

5. _____

BIBLE RHYMLE

A BIBLE RHYMLE is a pair of words that rhyme, have the same number of syllables, and fit a given definition.

EXAMPLES: Quiet Bible song is a **calm psalm**.

Maximillian's dues are **Max's taxes**.

1. burglars' sorrows _____

2. bullrush baby's flowers _____

3. Egyptian ruler's large foot appendages _____

4. a daughter-in-law molar _____

5. lion tamer's handbooks _____

6. lightless boat _____

7. bird sanctuary _____

8. good looking payment _____

9. hollow-middle tree _____

10. wax-light grip _____

11. improved epistle _____

12. lanky first king _____

13. missionary yell _____

14. improper sandal _____

15. patient man's garments _____

16. not deranged murderer _____

17. defrauder fisherman _____

18. water vessel trench _____

19. Cain's brother's telegrams _____

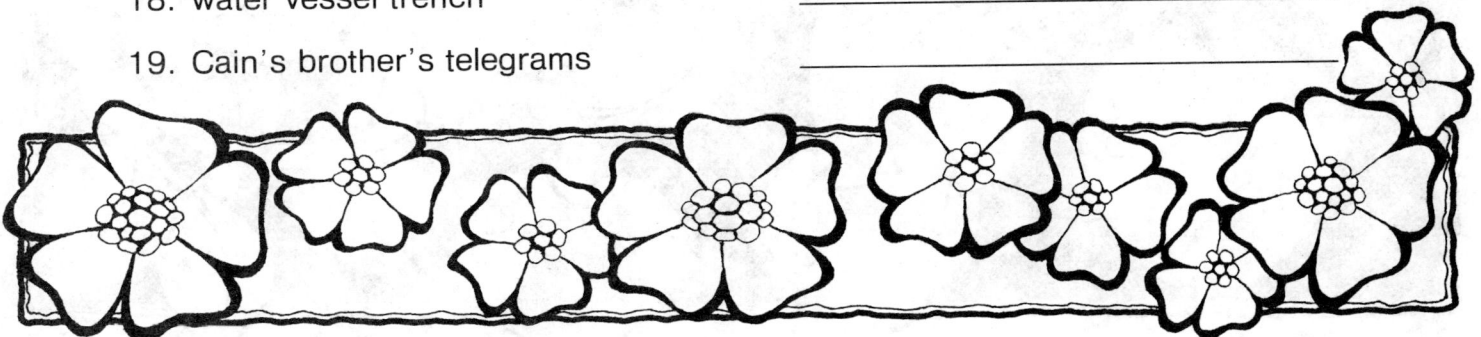

BIBLE RHYMLE

A BIBLE RHYMLE is a pair of words that rhyme, have the same number of syllables, and fit a given definition.

1. Samuel's mother's wilderness food   _____

2. caring bird   _____

3. large Bible fruit   _____

4. fame tale   _____

5. flame wailer   _____

6. red-fluid water disaster   _____

7. Italian city house   _____

8. tardy portal   _____

9. Italian performer   _____

10. nocturnal escape   _____

11. sad cat   _____

12. distant solar light   _____

13. cavern tomb   _____

14. alien crib   _____

15. shipbuilder snake   _____

MUSICAL CONNECTIONS

A MUSICAL CONNECTION is a code in which each note stands for its letter name. The notes spell out words in code form.

EXAMPLE:

Don't **feed** the animals.

KEY:

E F G A B C D E F

Use the key provided to decode the MUSICAL CONNECTIONS given below. Then make up some puzzles of your own.

1. David was an ___ ___ ___ marksman.

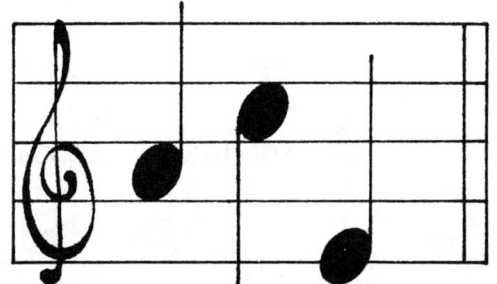

2. This is the ___ ___ ___ of grace.

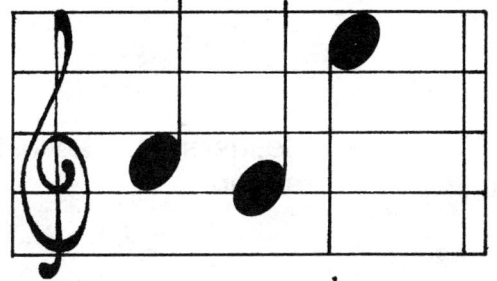

3. When Goliath was stabbed, then he was ___ ___ ___ ___ ___.

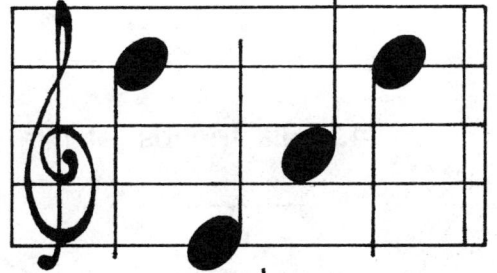

4. They spit in Christ's ___ ___ ___ ___.

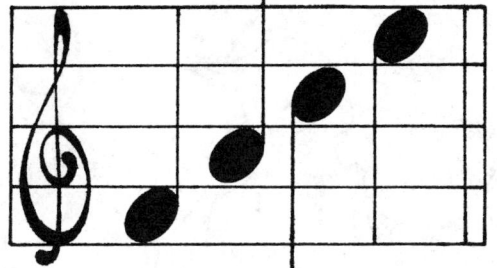

MUSICAL CONNECTIONS

A MUSICAL CONNECTION is a code in which each note stands for its letter name. The notes spell out words in code form.

Use the key provided on page 11 to decode the MUSICAL CONNECTIONS given below.

1. Another word for lions' den is _ _ _ _.

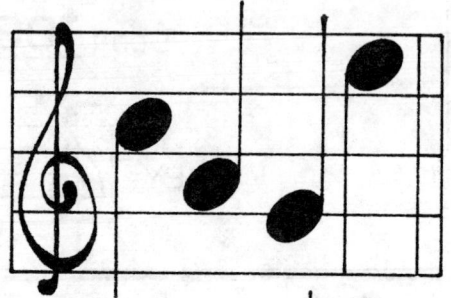

2. The man who could not hear was _ _ _ _.

3. Jesus said, "Lovest thou me . . . _ _ _ _ _ my sheep."

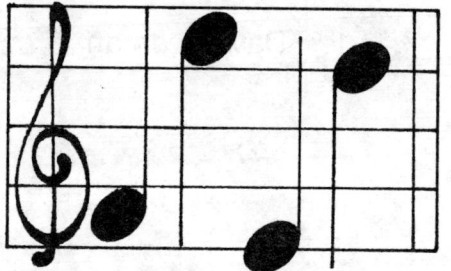

4. His friends let him down through the roof on his

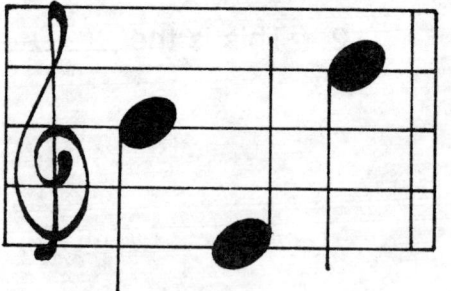

    _ _ _.

SQUARE CONNECTIONS

SQUARE CONNECTIONS are word puzzles in the shape of a square. To solve the puzzle, find where the eight-letter word begins, fill in the empty box with the correct missing letter, and write the word on the blank.

EXAMPLE:

```
I A H
M   N     = Nehemiah
E   E
```

These squares are all Christian characteristics.

```
N   A        C E P          A D
S   T        N   A        E   I
S E N        E   T        C N A
```
_____   _____   _____

```
Y M A        M E          E S S
T   T        S   K        N   G
  R U        S E N        D O
```
_____   _____   _____

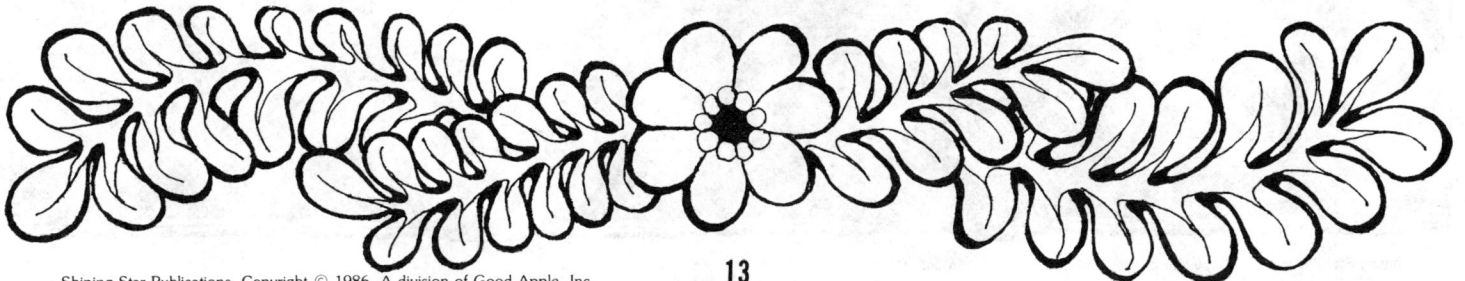

SQUARE CONNECTIONS

SQUARE CONNECTIONS are word puzzles in the shape of a square. To solve the puzzle, find where the eight-letter word begins, fill in the empty box with the correct missing letter, and write the word on the blank.

These squares are all occupations of Bible people.

	U	S
N	I	
A	I	C

R	F	U
E		M
R		E

O	R	S
T		C
P	L	

_____

E		B
R		A
E	M	L

_____

S	M	A
	N	
R	E	H

_____

E	R	
H		S
P	E	H

_____

WORDLE EPISTLE

A WORDLE EPISTLE uses shapes and positions of letters and groups of words to help convey a message.

EXAMPLE:

We don't <u>stand</u> a <u>words</u>.
play
all

We don't all understand a play on words.

Read this WORDLE EPISTLE from a youth director to a pastor.
Write the message correctly on a separate sheet of paper.

Dear Pastor <u>seer</u>:
or

Your church <u>looked</u> when we did our survey. It was merely sight. <u>We</u> you have many
was
an stand

young people who <u>average</u> in Bible knowledge.
are

Please send me a list of your young people, but <u>look</u> any possibilities as you review <u>all</u>
don't
your

list. It would be helpful if you <u>would</u> <u>sixteen</u>. Maybe we could help them <u>come</u> some of
line those
to

sensitive personalities <u>and</u> memory skills. It would also help if you would circle those
their developed

that you feel <u>committed</u>.
are

I have been <u>time</u> to select these teams, because we are <u>worked</u>, but conditions we
working
staffed and these

<u>react</u>.
often

Two times during our travels this summer the team will <u>night</u> as a group in a church
stay

fellowship hall. This tour is <u>due</u>, but I'm sure we <u>power</u> the host teams.
long
won't

This is an <u>important</u> for the team and me, but we have managed to keep <u>head</u> low
taking
the

and hopefully didn't <u>our</u> needs. The van may be a crowded the first week, so pray that
estimate
little

as we go up the mountains it <u>heat</u>.
doesn't

We don't want the fun <u>shadow</u> our main purpose, to know and God's Word and <u>to</u> the
to
stand
score

need <u>come</u> complacency in the reading of the Bible. I will <u>whelmed</u> if you send this to
to
be

<u>the</u> weekend. We <u>come</u> !
me
shall

WORDLE EPISTLE

A WORDLE EPISTLE uses shapes and positions of letters and groups of words to help convey a message.

Example: We don't <u>stand</u>.
all

<u>A play</u>
words.

Answers: We don't all understand.
A play on words.

Read this WORDLE EPISTLE from John Mark to Paul. Write the message correctly in the space below.

Dear Paul,

am   I
I joyed if what <u>heard</u> is correct. <u>stand</u>
                                              I

you are no longer <u>ground.</u> I'm sure you
     been   traveling
have cautious in the past, but <u>estimate</u>
                            don't

those you associate with who <u>mine</u> your
                         might
ministry by <u>handed</u> in their dealings.
         being   am
Please don't <u>stand</u> and think I reacting.
           miss   <u>that</u>   <u>can</u>
These things are <u>cover</u> night they power
  Don't   so   us
you. <u>look</u> taking time to write to <u>seas</u>,
                             an
although I'm sure it's been <u>sight</u> to this

point.

               Don't
               do,

                    John Mark

HIDDEN NAMES

A HIDDEN NAME of a Bible woman can be found by joining letters from different words to form the spelling of that name. The letters will appear in the proper order.

EXAMPLE: Monkeys have very entertaining mannerisms.

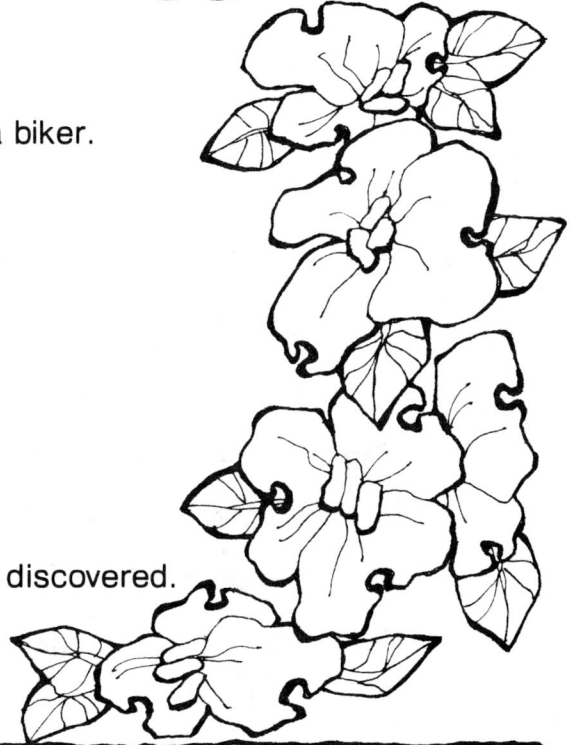

1. Water will mar that table surface.

2. The huge rut has possibilities of being trouble for a biker.

3. The baker told Grandma, ''Rye bread is on sale.''

4. Hello is a common greeting.

5. The lea had many fragrant wildflowers.

6. Put the peaches there in that bushel basket.

7. An expert mariner can navigate in a violent storm.

8. The peculiar ache lasted only seconds.

9. The case was unsolved until suddenly diaries were discovered.

10. A purple velvet cloak completed the outfit.

Think of some other women in the Bible and make your own HIDDEN NAME sentences.

1. _____

2. _____

3. _____

4. _____

5. _____

HIDDEN NAMES

A HIDDEN NAME of a Bible man can be found by joining letters from different words to form the spelling of that name. The letters will appear in the proper order.

EXAMPLE: Ada made a speech to the crowd.

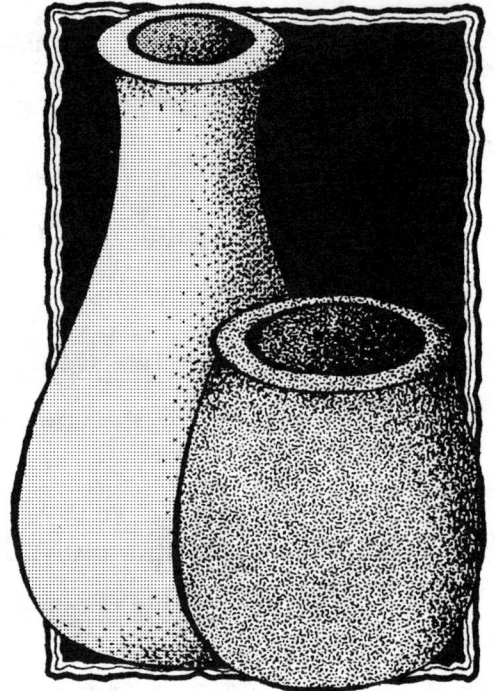

1. Dynamo sessions begin at two o'clock.

2. Please—No Children Allowed!

3. Give me the simple life!

4. The boa zipped through the grass.

5. Nonalcoholic ale beats turpentine for removing paint.

6. Use a sack for a Halloween mask.

7. The clever lad amused the king with his magical tricks.

8. The party started with the sound of a bell.

9. Nothing is as pesky as a mosquito.

10. The motel is half full tonight.

Think of some other men in the Bible and make your own HIDDEN NAME sentences.

1. _____

2. _____

3. _____

4. _____

5. _____

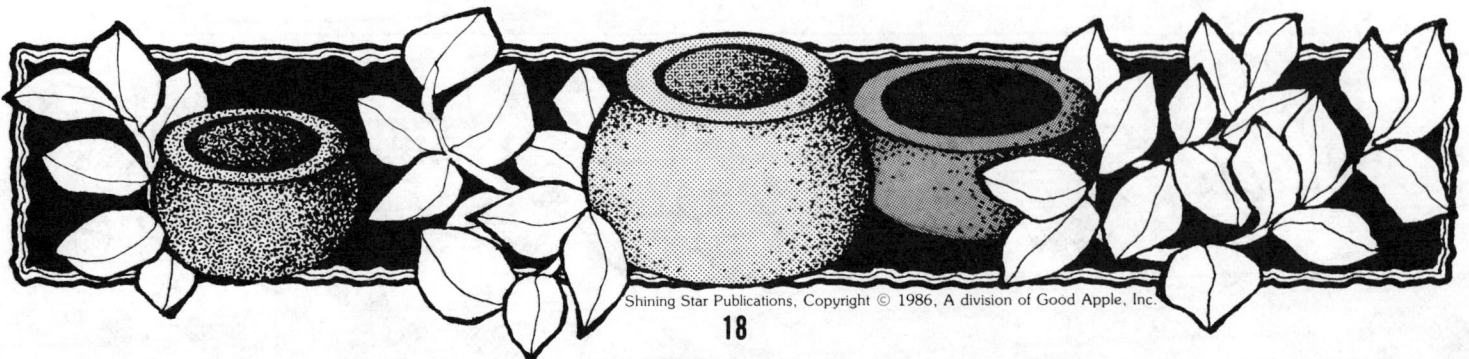

Shining Star Publications, Copyright © 1986, A division of Good Apple, Inc.

COMMON CONNECTIONS

The correct answer to each set of clues found below contains the common word *IN*. Example: Joseph's youngest brother: Benjam*IN*.

1. A sign of God's promise to Noah _____

2. Transgression _____

3. The name of the mountain where the Ten Commandments were given to Moses is

   _____

4. Three _____

5. Seven foolish _____

6. Moving air _____

7. To pour or rub oil on a person _____

8. Chastisement _____

9. Religious principle _____

10. Forevermore_____

11. Scarcity of food _____

12. Wise man's gift _____

13. Divine thought _____

14. Domain _____

The correct answer to each set of clues found below contains the common word *AN*. Example: Samuel's mother: *HAN*nah.

1. Wilderness food _____

2. They crucified Christ. _____

3. False pride _____

4. God's promise of blessing_____

5. Death method-Absolam _____

6. Land of milk and honey _____

7. New Testament book before Thessalonians _____

8. Lion tamer_____

9. New Testament book before Ephesians_____

10. Mankind_____

Shining Star Publications, Copyright © 1986, A division of Good Apple, Inc.

COMMON CONNECTIONS

The correct answer to each set of clues found below contains the common word *IS*. Example: Act of betrayal: k*IS*s.

1. Sanctimonious, hypocritical Jewish leader _____

2. Assurance _____

3. Food for five thousand _____

4. Solomon's gift _____

5. What to do to temptation _____

6. Jesus _____

7. Purification by water _____

8. The past _____

9. Major Old Testament prophet _____

10. Follower _____

11. Opposite of "in the tomb" _____

The correct answer to each set of clues found below contains the common word *ON*. Example: In agreement: c*ON*cur.

1. Musical tune _____

2. Male offspring _____

3. Synonym for rock _____

4. New Testament book after Colossians _____

5. Suffering _____

6. The bread and the cup _____

7. Fifth book of the Bible _____

8. Natural sweetener _____

9. Bring into harmony _____

10. Vegetable in the leek family _____

QUANTITATIVE CONNECTIONS

The correct answer to each set of clues found below has something to do with forty years. Fill in the blank with the person or persons who will make each statement correct.

1. _____ was forty when Rebekah married him.

2. _____ was forty when sent to spy in Canaan.

3. _____ known for wisdom ruled Israel forty years.

4. _____, Israel's first king, ruled forty years.

5. _____, the priest with whom Samuel lived, judged Israel forty years.

6. _____ ate manna for forty years in the wilderness.

7. _____ could not build a temple during his forty-year rule, since he was a man of war.

8. _____ did right in the sight of the Lord during his forty years of rule.

Each of the clues below contains a reference to forty days. Fill in the blank with the name of the person or persons who make the statement correct.

1. _____ was in the ark forty days.

2. _____, the giant, went before the Israelites forty days looking for a fight.

3. _____ went to Nineveh to warn the wicked to repent or be destroyed in forty days.

4. _____ saw Jesus forty days after He arose.

5. _____ fasted forty days in the wilderness before being tempted by Satan.

6. _____ was fed by the angels and had strength for forty days and nights.

7. _____ spied in the Promised Land forty days.

8. _____ was given the Ten Commandments while he spent forty days on the mountain.

QUANTITATIVE CONNECTIONS

The answer to each of the clues found below is the name of one of the twelve disciples.

1. The "Zealot" _____

2. Brought his brother to Jesus _____

3. The doubter _____

4. Did not like Nazareth _____

5. Tax collector _____

6. Brought Nathanael to Jesus _____

7. Lebbaeus _____

8. Took Judas' place _____

9. Betrayed Jesus _____

10. Denied Christ _____

11. Son of Alphaeus _____

12. Banned to Patmos _____

In each of the Bible verses listed below, find the name of one of the twelve sons of Jacob. Can you identify all twelve?

1. Genesis 35:18 _____

2. Genesis 30:24 _____

3. Genesis 30:11 _____

4. Genesis 30:8 _____

5. Genesis 30:20 _____

6. Genesis 29:32 _____

7. Genesis 29:33 _____

8. Genesis 30:18 _____

9. Genesis 30:13 _____

10. Genesis 29:35 _____

11. Genesis 30:6 _____

12. Genesis 29:34 _____

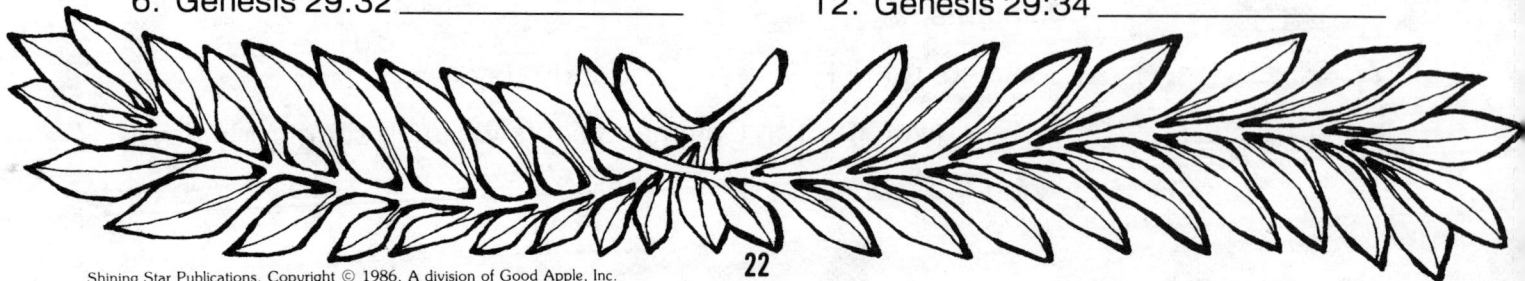

QUANTITATIVE CONNECTIONS

The answer to each of the clues found below all have something to do with the number four.

1. Four Gospels _____, _____,
   _____, _____

2. Four wives of David _____, _____,
   _____, _____

3. Men who refused to eat the king's food _____, _____,
   _____, _____

4. Four gifts to the prodigal son _____, _____,
   _____, _____

5. Four men in Nebuchadnezzar's furnace _____, _____,
   _____, _____

6. First four words of the Bible _____, _____,
   _____, _____

7. First four books of the Bible _____, _____,
   _____, _____

8. Four major prophets _____, _____,
   _____, _____

The answers to the clues found below are things found in groups of seven.

1. Revelation 17:9 _____

2. Revelation 12:3 _____

3. Revelation 4:5 _____

4. Revelation 5:6 _____

5. Revelation 5:1 _____

6. Revelation 1:12 _____

7. Revelation 5:6 _____

8. Revelation 17:9 _____

9. Revelation 15:1 _____

10. Revelation 1:4 _____

11. Revelation 12:3 _____

12. Revelation 17:10 _____

ALPHABET CONNECTIONS

An ALPHABET CONNECTION is one in which one letter in the code stands for another letter of the alphabet.

ALPHABET REVERSAL CODE KEY

LETTER: A B C D E F G H I J K L M N O P Q R S T U V W X Y Z
CODE: Z Y X W V U T S R Q P O N M L K J I H G F E D C B A

EXAMPLE:
CODED MESSAGE: GSRH DROO YV UFM!
DECODED MESSAGE: THIS WILL BE FUN!

A. Below you will find NAMES OF THE LORD in code. Use the code above to decode the message. Scripture references are given so you may check your answers.

1. DZB _____ John 14:6

2. ERMV _____ John 15:1

3. FMHKVZPZYOV TRUG _____ 2 Cor. 9:15

4. GIFGS _____ John 14:6

5. TLLW HSVKSVIW _____ John 10:11

6. HZERLFI LU GSV DLIOW _____ I John 4:14

B. Now look up the following Scriptures and, using the same key, write out in coded message the NAME OF THE LORD used in each verse.

1. Luke 2:11 _____ 2. John 1:29 _____

3. Dan. 9:25 _____ 4. Heb. 12:2 _____

Shining Star Publications, Copyright © 1986, A division of Good Apple, Inc.

ALPHABET CONNECTIONS

In this ALPHABET CONNECTION, one number in the code stands for another letter of the alphabet.

EXAMPLE:

KEY

1	2	3	4	5	6	7	8	9	10	11	12	13	14	15	16	17	18	19	20	21	22	23	24	25	26
A	B	C	D	E	F	G	H	I	J	K	L	M	N	O	P	Q	R	S	T	U	V	W	X	Y	Z

CODED MESSAGE: 20 8 9 19   9 19   6 21 14!

DECODED MESSAGE: THIS   IS   FUN!

A. Using the code above to decode the messages, find the NAMES OF THE LORD. Scripture references are given so you may check your answers.

1. ___ ___ ___ ___ ___   ___ ___   ___ ___ ___   ___ ___ ___ ___ ___
    12 9 7 8 20   15 6   20 8 5   23 15 18 12 4   John 8:12

2. ___ ___ ___ ___   ___ ___   ___ ___ ___   ___ ___ ___ ___ ___ ___ ___
    12 9 12 25   15 6   20 8 5   22 1 12 12 5 25 19   Song of Sol. 2:1

3. ___ ___ ___   ___ ___   ___ ___ ___ ___ ___ ___ ___
    13 1 14   15 6   19 15 18 18 15 23 19   Isaiah 53:3

4. ___ ___ ___ ___ ___ ___   ___ ___   ___ ___ ___ ___ ___
    16 18 9 14 3 5   15 6   16 5 1 3 5   Isaiah 9:6

5. ___ ___ ___ ___ ___ ___ ___ ___ ___ ___ ___ ___
    18 5 19 21 18 18 5 3 20 9 15 14   John 11:25

6. ___ ___ ___ ___   ___ ___   ___ ___ ___ ___ ___ ___
    18 15 19 5   15 6   19 8 1 18 15 14   Song of Sol. 2:1

B. Now look up the following Scriptures and, using the same key, write out in coded message the NAME OF THE LORD used in each verse.

1. Acts 10:36 _____   2. I John 5:13 _____

3. Isaiah 9:6 _____   4. Luke 1:32 _____

CRYPTIC QUOTES

A CRYPTIC QUOTE is a mystery message revealed through using defined words as clues. Each number in the defined word represents a letter. The letters of the defined words are then matched to numbered spaces that spell out the quote. Fill in the blanks in each statement. Then fill in the quote at the bottom.

EXAMPLE:

3-10-6-7 is the bird Noah sent from the ark.

$$\frac{D}{3}\ \frac{O}{10}\ \frac{V}{6}\ \frac{E}{7}$$

4-2-1-8 is what Abraham used to build the altar.

$$\frac{L}{4}\ \frac{O}{2}\ \frac{G}{1}\ \frac{S}{8}$$

9-5-11 is the opposite of "me."

$$\frac{Y}{9}\ \frac{O}{5}\ \frac{U}{11}$$

$$\frac{G}{1}\ \frac{O}{2}\ \frac{D}{3}\quad \frac{L}{4}\ \frac{O}{5}\ \frac{V}{6}\ \frac{E}{7}\ \frac{S}{8}\quad \frac{Y}{9}\ \frac{O}{10}\ \frac{U}{11}$$

---

1. The 15-7-17-19-12-8-20 is where plays are presented.

$$\overline{15}\ \overline{7}\ \overline{17}\overline{19}\overline{12}\ \overline{8}\ \overline{20}$$

2. 14-11-13-3-6 is what Ivory soap will do.

$$\overline{14}\overline{11}\overline{13}\ \overline{3}\ \overline{6}$$

3. A 22-2-10-4-21 is a symbol of Valentine's Day.

$$\overline{22}\ \overline{2}\ \overline{10}\ \overline{4}\ \overline{21}$$

4. 16-5 is the opposite of "she."

$$\overline{16}\ \overline{5}$$

5. 1-18-9 is the answer we want to most requests.

$$\overline{1}\ \overline{18}\ \overline{9}$$

$$\overline{1}\ \overline{2}\quad \overline{3}\ \overline{4}\ \overline{5}\quad \overline{6}\ \overline{7}\ \overline{8}\quad \overline{9}\ \overline{10}\overline{11}\overline{12}\quad \overline{13}\overline{14}\quad \overline{15}\overline{16}\overline{17}\quad \overline{18}\overline{19}\overline{20}\overline{21}\overline{22}$$

1. 8-2 is the opposite of "stop."

$$\overline{8}\ \overline{2}$$

2. A 6-7-3 is what fits on the top of a jar.

$$\overline{6}\ \overline{7}\ \overline{3}$$

3. 5-4-1-9-10 is the sense of vision.

$$\overline{5}\ \overline{4}\ \overline{1}\ \overline{9}\ \overline{10}$$

$$\overline{1}\ \overline{2}\ \overline{3}\quad \overline{4}\ \overline{5}\quad \overline{6}\ \overline{7}\ \overline{8}\ \overline{9}\ \overline{10}$$

CRUCIAL CONNECTIONS

CRUCIAL CONNECTIONS is a puzzle that is solved simply by counting letters in words and fitting the proper word into the proper place on a grid. This puzzle has the words *SHOEMAKER* and *EMBALMER* filled in to help you get started. All the words in this puzzle are types of craftsmen and workmen in the Bible.

Use these words:

5 Letters	6 Letters	7 Letters	8 Letters	9 Letters
Mason	Miller	Artisan	Gardener	Carpenter
Baker	Carver	Jeweler	Embalmer	Goldsmith
	Weaver			Shoemaker
	Tailor			

10 Letters

Apothecary

11 Letters

Silversmith
Shipbuilder

Shining Star Publications, Copyright © 1986, A division of Good Apple, Inc.

CRUCIAL CONNECTIONS

CRUCIAL CONNECTIONS is a puzzle that is solved simply by counting letters in words and fitting the proper word into the proper place on a grid. This puzzle has the word *METHUSELAH* already filled in to help you get started. All the words in this puzzle are names of Old Testament personalities.

Use these words:

3 Letters	4 Letters	5 Letters	6 Letters	7 Letters
Eve	Noah	Enoch	Joseph	Abraham
Lot	Adam	Sarah	Rachel	Rebekah
	Cain	David	Salome	Solomon
	Abel	Isaac	Esther	
	Levi	Moses	Hannah	
	Seth	Herod		
	Leah			

9 Letters	10 Letters
Elizabeth	Methuselah

ROUND ABOUT "THE WORD"

Each circle contains a book of the Old Testament in puzzle form. The letters may appear in varied positions, and frequently the outside circle is the letter *O*.

1._____

2._____

3._____

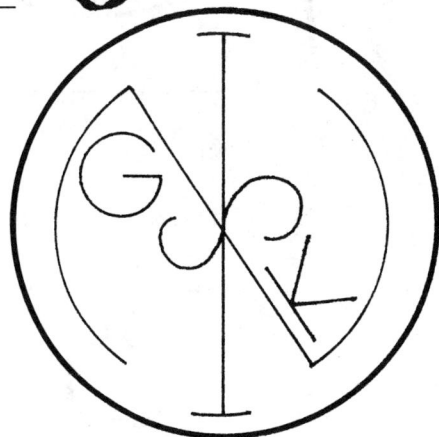

4._____

5._____

ROUND ABOUT "THE WORD"

Each circle contains a book of the Old Testament in puzzle form. The letters may appear in varied positions, and frequently the outside circle is the letter *O*.

1._____

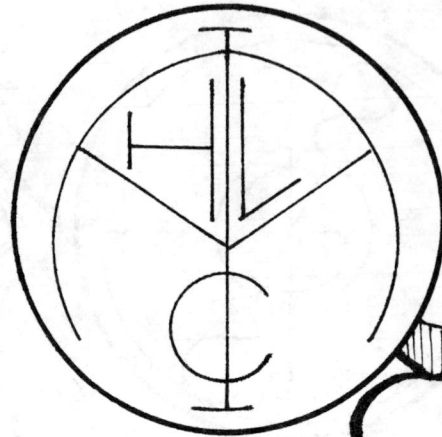

2._____

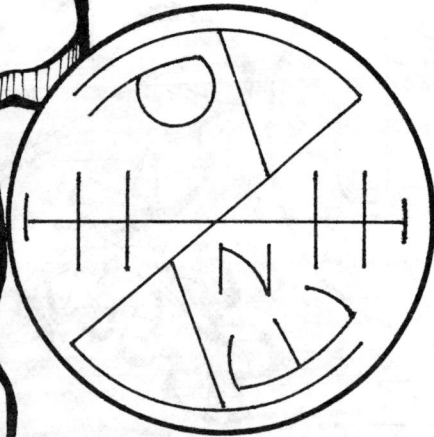

3._____

4._____

ROUND ABOUT "THE WORD"

Each circle contains a book of the Old Testament in puzzle form. The letters may appear in varied positions, and frequently the outside circle is the letter *O*.

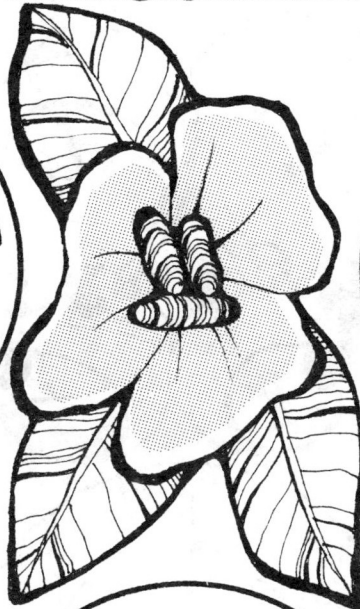

1._____

2._____

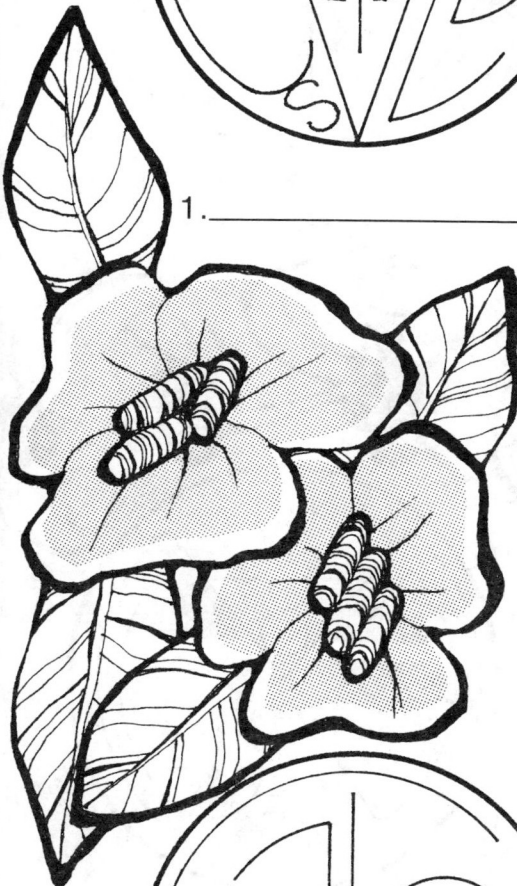

3._____

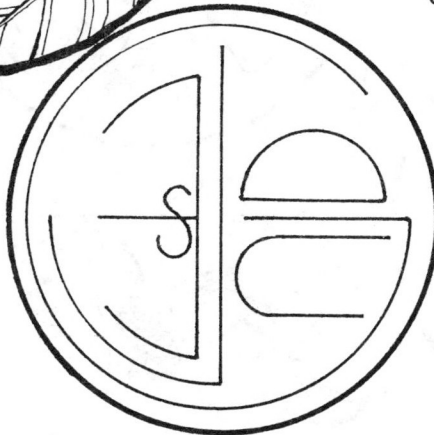
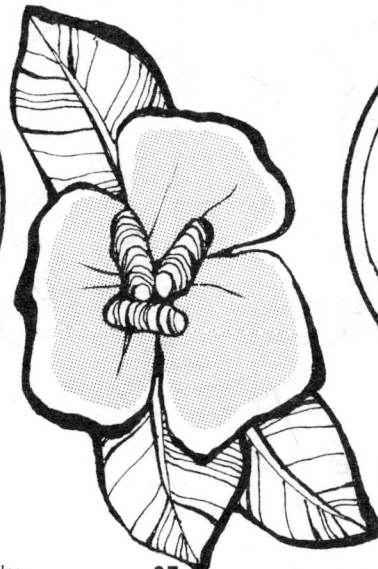

4._____

5._____

ROUND ABOUT "THE WORD"

Each circle contains a book of the New Testament in puzzle form. The letters may appear in varied positions, and frequently the outside circle is the letter O.

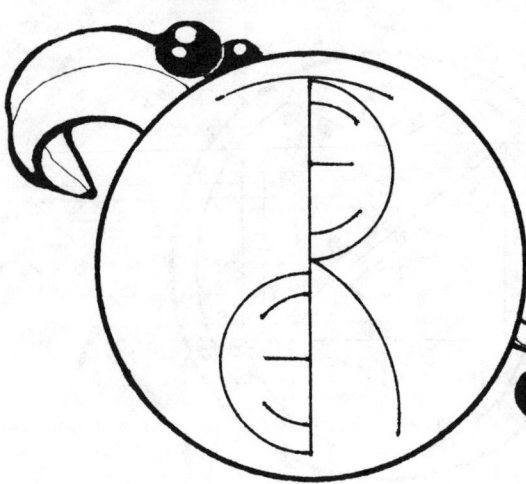

1._____

2._____

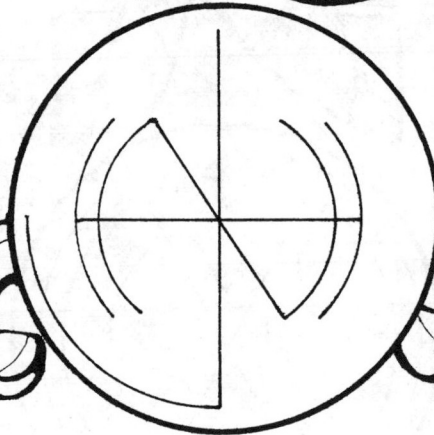

3._____

4._____

5._____

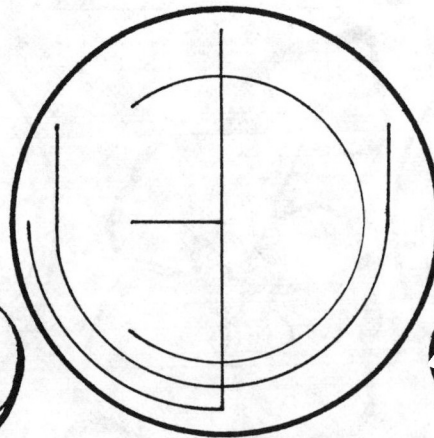

6._____

ROUND ABOUT "THE WORD"

Each circle contains a book of the New Testament in puzzle form. The letters may appear in varied positions, and frequently the outside circle is the letter O.

1._____

2._____

3._____

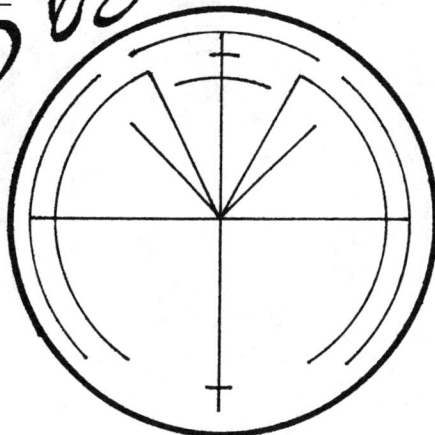

4._____

5._____

39

ROUND ABOUT "THE WORD"

Each circle contains a book of the New Testament in puzzle form. The letters may appear in varied positions, and frequently the outside circle is the letter O.

1._____

2._____

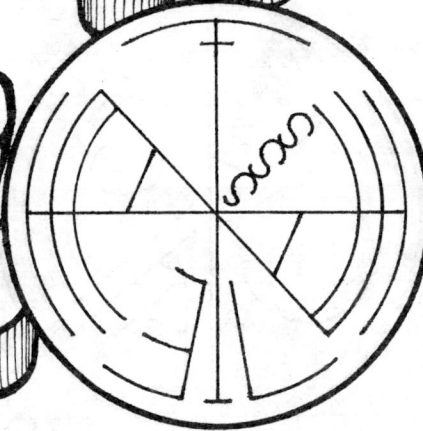

3._____

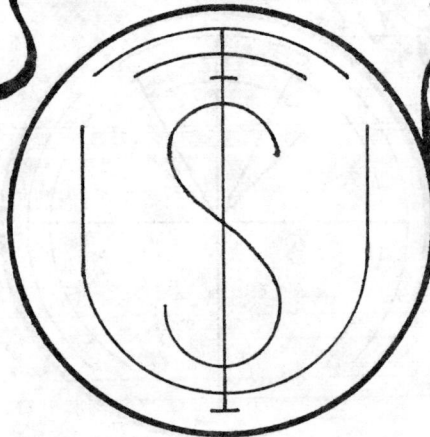

4._____

5._____

ROUND ABOUT "THE WORD"

Each circle contains a book of the New Testament in puzzle form. The letters may appear in varied positions, and frequently the outside circle is the letter O.

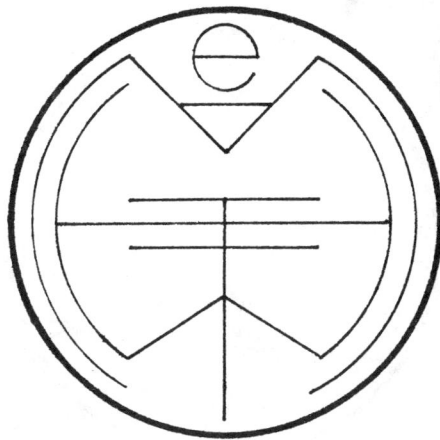 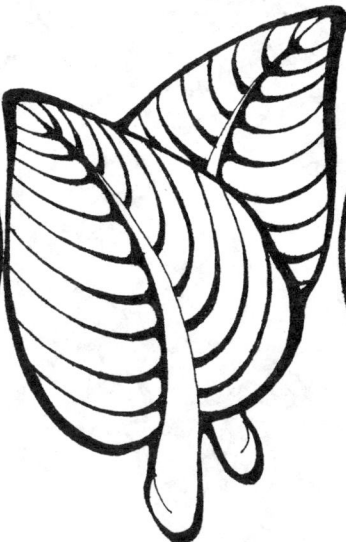 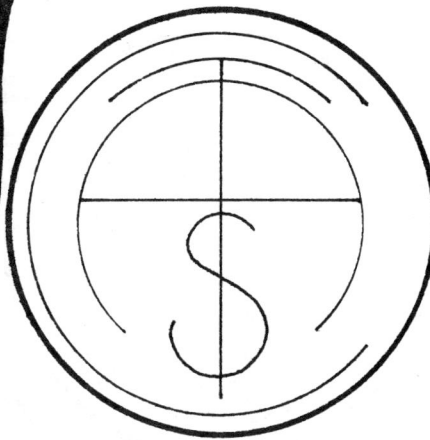

1._____   2._____

 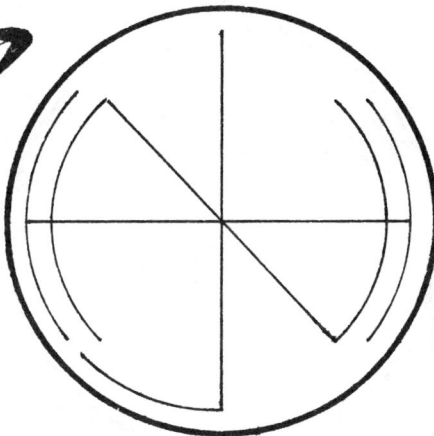 

3._____

 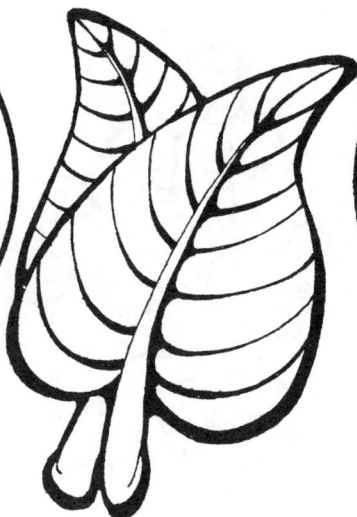 

4._____   5._____

ROUND ABOUT "THE WORD"

Create your own "Round About 'the Word'" puzzles in the circles found below. You may want to choose biblical names. Show your puzzles to a friend and see if he/she can figure out each one.

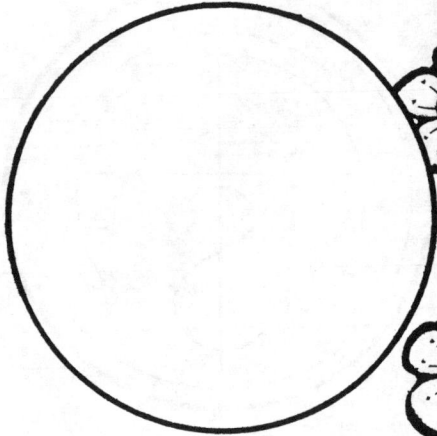
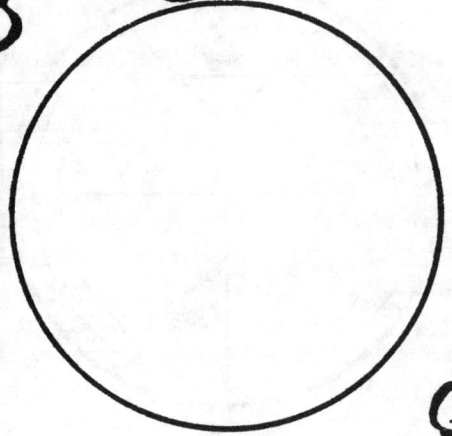

1._____

2._____

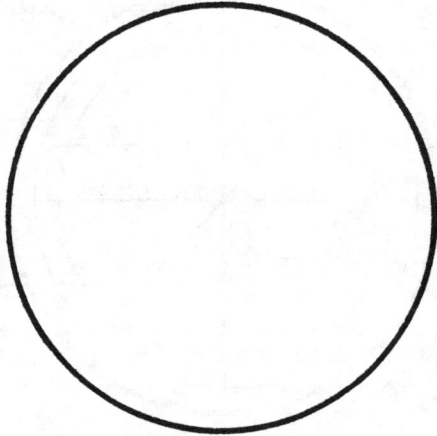

3._____

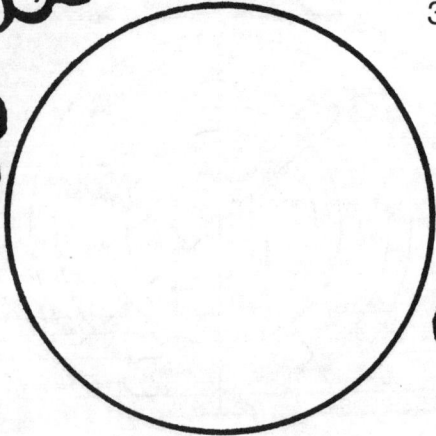
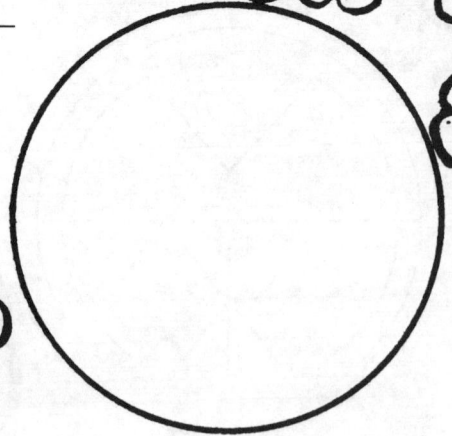

4._____

5._____

42

ANSWER KEY

BIBLE WORDLES p. 5
1. Saved by Grace 2. Power over Sin 3. Life after Death 4. Cornerstone 5. Daniel in the Lions' Den 6. The Last Supper

BIBLE WORDLES p. 6
1. Kneel Before Him 2. Holy Bible 3. Rock of Ages 4. Missionary Overseas 5. Pray Before Every Meal 6. Sunday 7. Bible Reading Before Bed 8. Morning Prayer 9. Noah's Ark

BIBLE WORDLES p. 7
1. Abide with Me 2. Nothing But the Blood 3. Oh, Happy Day 4. Standing on the Promises 5. Grace Greater Than Our Sin 6. The Solid Rock

BIBLE WORDLES p. 8
1. Just Like His Great Love 2. Count Your Blessings 3. In My Heart There Rings a Melody 4. Ring the Bells of Heaven 5. Higher Ground

BIBLE RHYMLE p. 9
1. thieves' grieves, 2. Moses' roses 3. Pharaoh's big toes 4. Ruth tooth 5. Daniel's manuals 6. dark ark 7. raven haven 8. handsome ransom 9. empty core Sycamore 10. candle handle 11. better letter 12. tall Saul 13. Paul call 14. wrong thong 15. Job's robes 16. sane Cain 17. cheater Peter 18. boat moat 19. Abel's cables

BIBLE RHYMLE p. 10
1. Hannah manna 2. love dove 3. big fig 4. glory story 5. fire crier 6. blood flood 7. Rome home 8. late gate 9. Roman showman 10. night flight 11. cryin' lion 12. far star 13. cave grave 14. stranger manger 15. Noah boa

MUSICAL CONNECTIONS p. 11
1. ace 2. age 3. dead 4. face

MUSICAL CONNECTIONS p. 12
1. cage 2. deaf 3. feed 4. bed

SQUARE CONNECTIONS p. 13

N	E	A		C	E	P		R	A	D
S		T		N		A		E		I
S	E	N		E	I	T		C	N	A

NEATNESS · PATIENCE · RADIANCE

Y	M	A		M	E	E		E	S	S
T		T		S		K		N		G
I	R	U		S	E	N		D	O	O

MATURITY · MEEKNESS · GOODNESS

SQUARE CONNECTIONS p. 14

M	U	S		R	F	U		O	R	S
N		I		E		M		T		C
A	I	C		P	R	E		P	L	U

MUSICIAN · PERFUMER · SCULPTOR

E	M	B		S	M	A		E	R	D
R		A		D		N		H		S
E	M	L		R	E	H		P	E	H

EMBALMER · HERDSMAN · SHEPHERD

WORDLE EPISTLE p. 15
Dear Pastor or Overseer:

Your church was overlooked when we did our survey. It was merely an oversight. We understand you have many young people who are above average in Bible knowledge.

Please send me a list of your young people, but don't overlook any possibilities as you review your overall list. It would be helpful if you would underline those over sixteen. Maybe we could help them to overcome some of their oversensitive personalities and underdeveloped memory skills. It would also help if you would circle those you feel are overcomitted.

I have been working overtime to select these teams, because we are understaffed and overworked, but under these conditions we often overreact.

Two times during our travels this summer the team will stay overnight as a group in a church fellowship hall. This tour is long overdue, but I'm sure we won't overpower the host teams.

This is an important undertaking for the team and me, but we have managed to keep the overhead low and hopefully didn't underestimate our needs. The van may be a little overcrowded the first week, so pray that as we go up the mountains it doesn't overheat.

We don't want the fun to overshadow our main purpose, to know and understand God's Word and to underscore the need to overcome complacency in the reading of the Bible. I will be overwhelmed if you send this to me over the weekend.

We shall overcome!

WORDLE EPISTLE p. 16
Dear Paul,

I am overjoyed if what I overheard is correct. I understand you are no longer traveling underground. I'm sure you have been overcautious in the past, but don't underestimate those you associate with who might undermine your ministry by being underhanded in their dealings.

Please don't misunderstand and think I am over-reacting. These things are so undercover that over-night they can overpower you. Don't overlook taking time to write to us overseas, although I'm sure it's been an oversight to this point.

Don't overdo,
John Mark

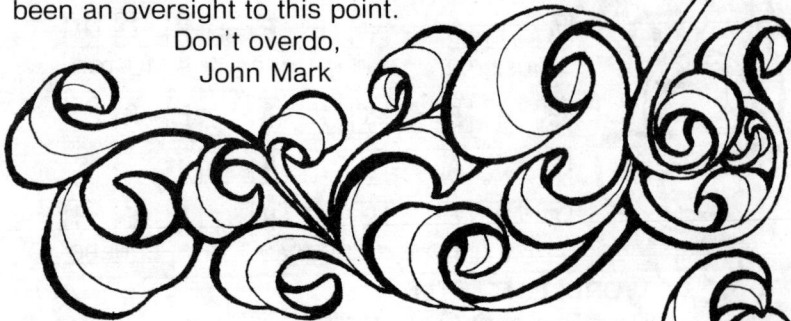

HIDDEN NAMES   p. 17
1. Martha 2. Ruth 3. Mary 4. Lois 5. Leah 6. Esther 7. Anna 8. Rachel 9. Lydia 10. Eve

HIDDEN NAMES   p. 18
1. Moses, Amos 2. Enoch 3. Eli 4. Boaz 5. Caleb 6. Asa 7. Adam 8. Abel 9. Asa, Amos 10. Elisha

COMMON CONNECTIONS   p. 19
1. rainbow 2. sin 3. Sinai 4. Trinity 5. virgins 6. wind 7. anoint 8. discipline 9. doctrine 10. everlasting (infinity) 11. famine 12. frankincense 13. inspiration 14. kingdom

1. manna 2. Romans 3. vanity 4. covenant 5. hanging 6. Canaan 7. Colossians 8. Daniel 9. Galatians 10. humanity

COMMON CONNECTIONS   p. 20
1. Pharisee 2. promise 3. fish 4. wisdom 5. resist 6. Christ 7. baptism 8. history 9. Isaiah 10. disciple 11. risen

1. song 2. son 3. stone 4. Thessalonians 5. agony 6. communion 7. Deuteronomy 8. honey 9. reconcile 10. onion

QUANTITATIVE CONNECTIONS   p. 21
1. Isaac 2. Joshua 3. Solomon 4. Saul 5. Eli 6. Israelites 7. David 8. Absalom

1. Noah 2. Goliath 3. Jonah 4. The Apostles 5. Jesus 6. Elijah 7. Caleb 8. Moses

QUANTITATIVE CONNECTIONS   p. 22
1. Simon 2. Andrew 3. Thomas 4. Nathanael 5. Matthew 6. Philip 7. Thaddaeus 8. Matthias 9. Judas 10. Peter 11. James 12. John

1. Benjamin 2. Joseph 3. Gad 4. Naphtali 5. Zebulun 6. Reuben 7. Simeon 8. Issachar 9. Asher 10. Judah 11. Dan 12. Levi

QUANTITATIVE CONNECTIONS   p. 23
1. Matthew, Mark, Luke, John 2. Abigail, Michal, Ahinoam, Bath-sheba 3. Daniel, Shadrach, Meshach, Abed-nego 4. robe, shoes, ring, fatted calf 5. Shadrach, Meshach, Abed-nego, man in white 6. In the beginning God 7. Genesis, Exodus, Leviticus, Numbers 8. Jeremiah, Isaiah, Ezekiel, Daniel

1. heads (or mountains) 2. heads (or crowns) 3. lamps 4. horns (or eyes) 5. seals 6. candlesticks 7. eyes (or horns) 8. mountains (or heads) 9. angels (or plagues) 10. spirits (or churches) 11. crowns (or heads) 12. kings

ALPHABET CONNECTIONS   p. 24
1. Way 2. Vine 3. Unspeakable Gift 4. Truth 5. Good Shepherd 6. Saviour of the World

1. Christ the Lord
   XSIRHG GSV OLIW
2. Lamb of God,
   OZNY LU TLW
3. Messiah
   NVHHRZS
4. Author, Finisher
   ZFGSLI, URMRHSVI

ALPHABET CONNECTIONS   p. 25
1. Light of the World 2. Lily of the Valleys 3. Man of Sorrows 4. Prince of Peace 5. Resurrection 6. Rose of Sharon

1. L O R D   O F   A L L
    12 15 18 4   15 6   1 12 12

2. S O N   O F   G O D
    19 15 14   15 6   7 15 4

3. C O U N S E L L O R   (Answers m
    3 15 21 14 19 5 12 12 15 18   vary.)

4. S O N   O F   T H E
    19 15 14   15 6   20 8 5

    H I G H E S T
    8 9 7 8 5 19 20

CRYPTIC QUOTES   p. 26
1. theater 2. float 3. heart 4. he 5. yes
YE ARE THE SALT OF THE EARTH
1. go 2. lid 3. sight
GOD IS LIGHT

CRYPTIC QUOTES   p. 27
1. hail 2. halt 3. off
HALL OF FAITH
1. fur 2. die 3. gorgeous
GOD IS OUR REFUGE

CRUCIAL CONNECTIONS p. 28
Nature/Battle could be interchanged.

BATTLE · PENITENCE · THANKSGIVING · TRUST · NATURE · ANGUISH · MESSIANIC · DESPAIR · MERCY · DEVOTION · SUFFERING · HISTORICAL · CAPTIVITY · VENGEANCE · ALPHABETIC · PRAISE

CRUCIAL CONNECTIONS p. 29

MILLER · MASON · JEWELER · WEAVER · APOTHECARY · ARTISAN · SHIPBUILDER · CARVER · SILVERSMITH · SHOEMAKER · BAKER · EMBALMER · CARPENTER · GOLDSMITH · TAILOR · GARDENER

CRUCIAL CONNECTIONS p. 30

MOSES · RACHEL · SETH · REBEKAH · LEAH · EVE · ANNE · HEROD · NOAH · SALOME · METHUSELAH · ABRAHAM · ELIZABETH · LOT · LEVI · ESTHER · ANNA · ISAAC · ABEL · JOSEPH · SOLOMON

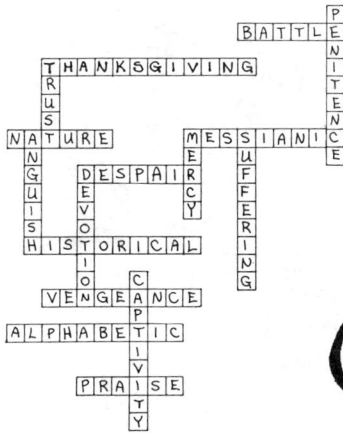

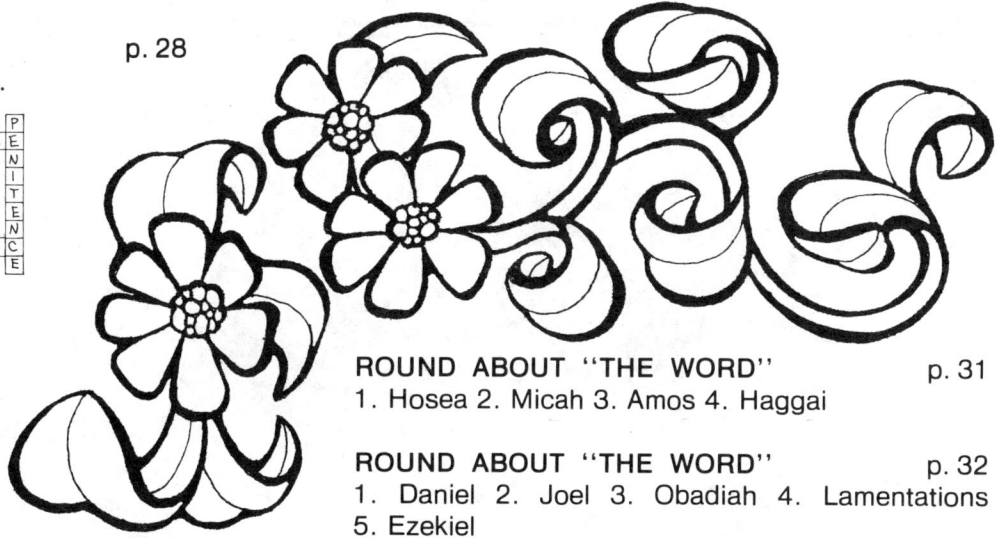

ROUND ABOUT "THE WORD" p. 31
1. Hosea 2. Micah 3. Amos 4. Haggai

ROUND ABOUT "THE WORD" p. 32
1. Daniel 2. Joel 3. Obadiah 4. Lamentations 5. Ezekiel

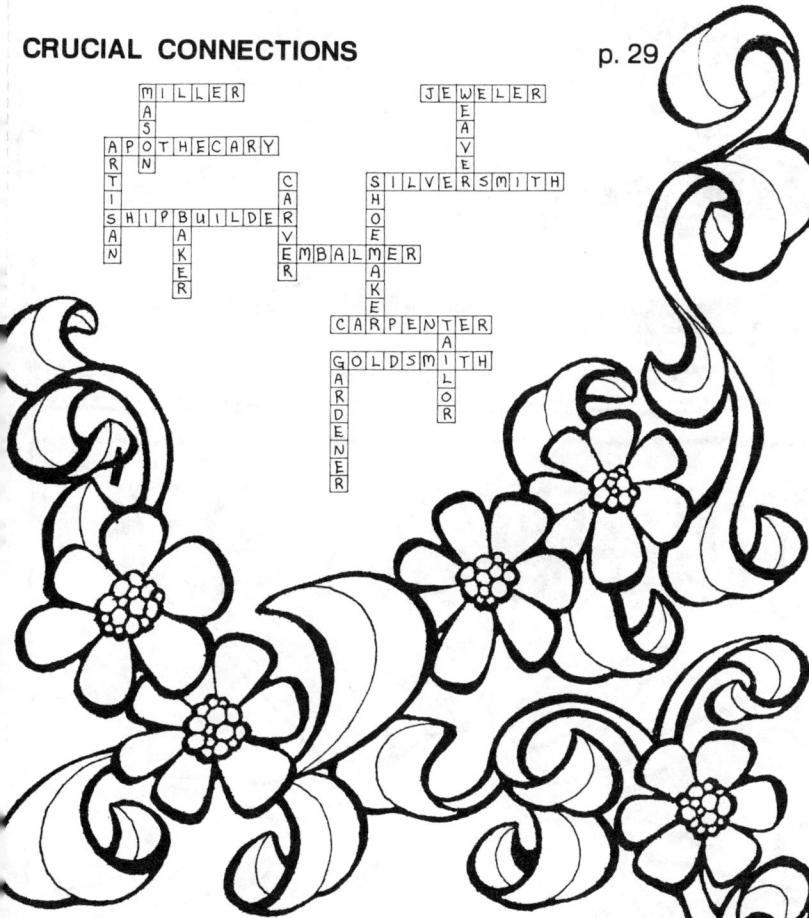

ROUND ABOUT "THE WORD" p. 33
1. Isaiah 2. Ezra 3. Psalms 4. Esther 5. Jeremiah

ROUND ABOUT "THE WORD" p. 34
1. Chronicles 2. Job 3. Ecclesiastes 4. Nehemiah 5. Proverbs

ROUND ABOUT "THE WORD" p. 35
1. Genesis 2. Deuteronomy 3. Joshua 4. Ruth 5. Kings

ROUND ABOUT "THE WORD" p. 36
1. Habakkuk 2. Malachi 3. Zephaniah 4. Zechariah

ROUND ABOUT "THE WORD" p. 37
1. Leviticus 2. Numbers 3. Samuel 4. Judges 5. Exodus

ROUND ABOUT "THE WORD" p. 38
1. Peter 2. Hebrews 3. John 4. Revelation 5. James 6. Jude

ROUND ABOUT "THE WORD" p. 39
1. Ephesians 2. Romans 3. Galatians 4. Luke 5. Timothy

ROUND ABOUT "THE WORD" p. 40
1. Colossians 2. Philippians 3. Thessalonians 4. Titus 5. Philemon

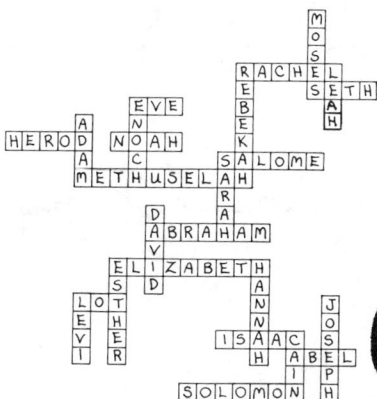

ROUND ABOUT "THE WORD" p. 41
1. Matthew 2. Acts 3. John 4. Mark 5. Corinthians

TO: _____ You're

Toadily Awesome as a Problem Solver

SIGNED: _____

I MADE THIS DEDUCKTION: YOU ARE A POWERFUL PUZZLER!

TO: _____   SIGNED: _____

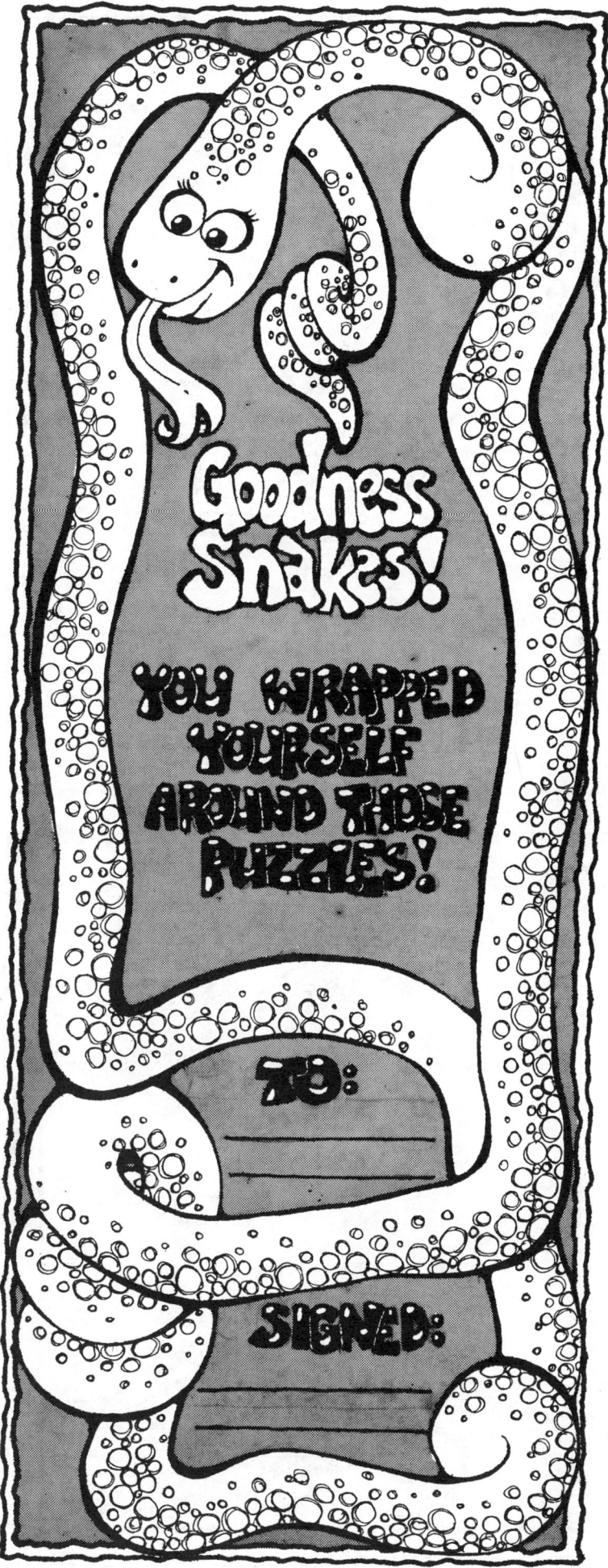

Goodness
Snakes!

YOU WRAPPED
YOURSELF
AROUND THOSE
PUZZLES!

TO:
_____

SIGNED:
_____
_____

YOU'RE A
NATURAL!

TO:
_____
SIGNED:
_____

Listen Up!
YOU'RE GREAT AT
PUZZLES!

TO:
_____
SIGNED:
_____

"BEAR" this in mind:
"You'll go "fur" in problem solving!"
TO:
SIGNED:

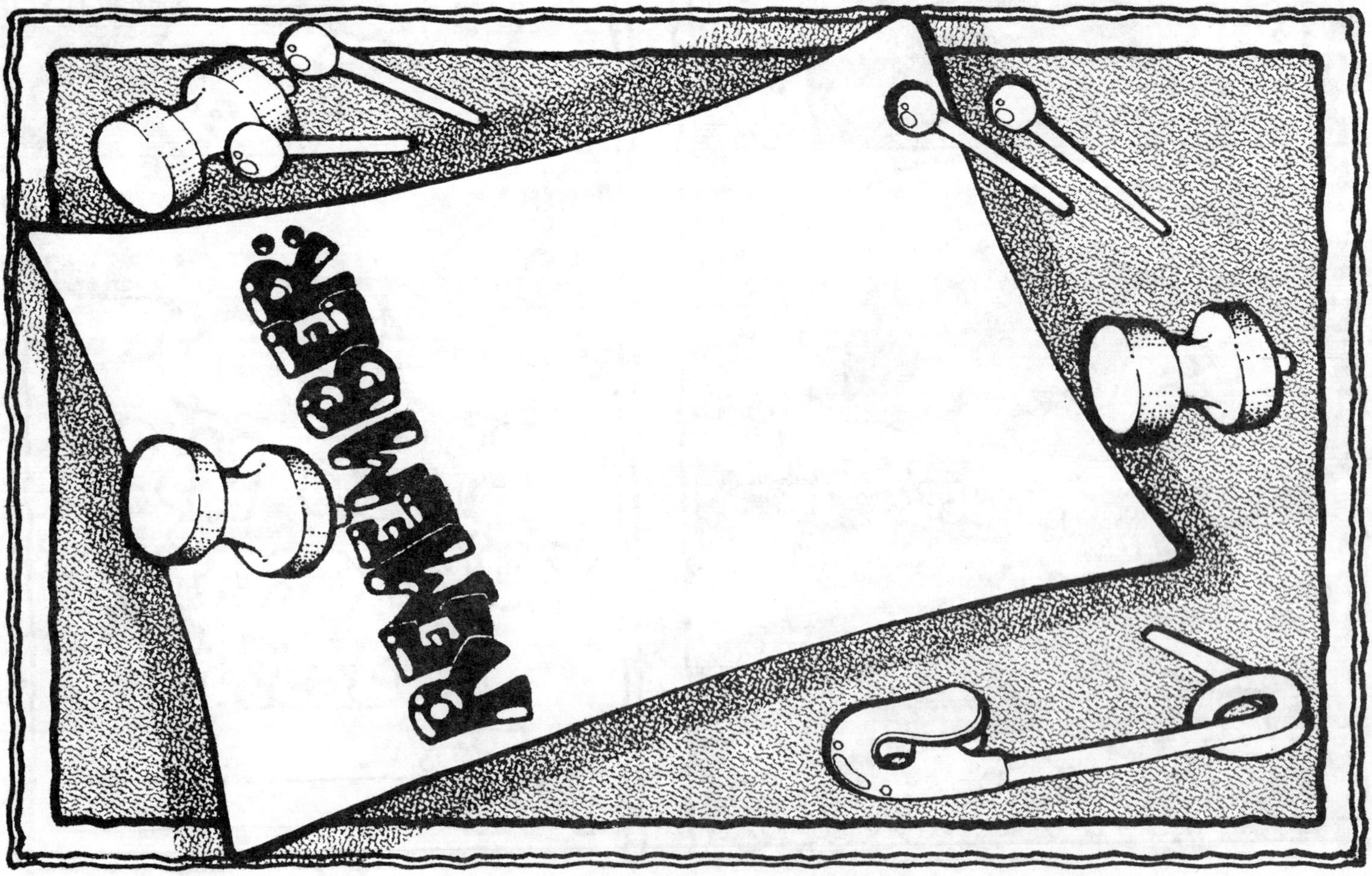
REMEMBER: